better together*

* This book is best read together, grownup and kid.

a
kids
book
about

a kids book about

BEING AUTHENTIC

by Amanda Seales

A Kids Book About
Editor Emma Wolf
Head of Design Rick DeLucco
Publisher Jelani Memory

DK
Senior Production Editor Jennifer Murray
Production Controller Joss Moore
Publisher Paula Regan
Publishing Director Mark Searle

This American Edition, 2026
Published in the United States by DK Publishing,
a Division of Penguin Random House LLC
1745 Broadway, 20th Floor, New York, NY 10019

26 27 28 29 10 9 8 7 6 5 4 3 2 1
001—357576—Oct/26

First published in Great Britain in 2026 by
Dorling Kindersley Limited, 20 Vauxhall Bridge Road, London SW1V 2SA
A Penguin Random House Company

The authorised representative in the EEA is
Dorling Kindersley Verlag GmbH. Arnulfstr. 124, 80636 Munich, Germany.

A CIP catalogue record for this book is available from the British Library

ISBN 978-0-2417-9963-5

Printed and bound in China

www.dk.com

akidsco.com

MIX
Paper
FSC™ C018179

Dedicated to my 1st and 2nd grade teachers,
Mrs. Channel and Mzzzzzz. Law-Bowman,
who saw my light and let it shine.

Intro
for grownups

Authenticity. Being true to yourself. Loving who you are. These are lifelong pursuits that are often so challenging to maintain. The older we get, and the more societal influence we're exposed to, the harder it is to stay strong in who we are.

Here's the great thing: Kids are pretty good at being their authentic selves.

It's often much later that different pressures and expectations to "fit in" and "be normal" arise. So, what's the best thing you, as a grownup who loves the kid(s) in your life, can do?

Encourage that authenticity. Celebrate their uniqueness. Cheer on their weirdness.

Being authentic makes us kinder, more curious, and more compassionate. And it's a really brave and wonderful thing to be.

When I was a kid,
hip-hop was everywhere,
and it was all about
keeping it real.

THAT'S WHAT
I'M HERE TO DO
WITH YOU!

In other words,
I'm going to teach
you all about what

BEING

AUTHENTIC means.

Society teaches us
to chase normalcy.

Normalcy means being unremarkable and just like everybody else.

But you might not be like everybody else, which is OK!

And actually...

it's necessary!

Imagine
if all the
flowers
were the
same color.

Imagine if all the clouds were the same shape.

What a boring, bland world we'd live in!

They're not supposed to be all the same, and neither are you.

Being authentic means to...

LIVE WHAT YOU FEEL ON THE INSIDE, ON THE OUTSIDE.

Regardless of whether it's different.

WHAT MATTERS
THAT YOU'RE THE

IS
REAL YOU.

Without lies,
without faking,
without pretending.

BEING AUTHEN

TIC IS HONEST.

I was always different.

Too loud.

Too short.

And I had too many feelings.

Sometimes, that was too much for my family, my friends, and my teachers.

Which sometimes felt like too much for me.

It made me feel like I needed to adjust and be a version of myself that they wanted, instead of who I really was.

I would try, but
it never worked.

I JUST COULDN'T FAKE IT.

It took a while to find the people
I didn't have to fake it with.

So, let's take it to high school.

I'm **really loud**,

really short,

and **really sensitive**.

And ***really*** **close** with
my best friend, Tara.

Then there was Jules.
And she was really close
with *her* best friend, Andrea.

Well, one day, Andrea turned to Jules and said,

"We don't mesh, I don't think we should be BFFs anymore."

And that very same day, Tara turned to me and said,

"We can't be BFFs anymore because you don't pluck* your eyebrows."

*My freshman year of college my friend Vanessa taught me how to pluck my eyebrows while sitting on the floor of her dorm room. To this day, I still pluck them the same way! What's funny is that the bushy eyebrows I had in high school are now the style! But what matters most isn't what's in style, it's about what feels good to you!

Julia and I found each other at lunch and cried over our sandwiches because we had both been dissed.

We did this for **WEEKS!**

Eating lunch together, hanging out, having sleepovers...talking about how our best friends had dropped us.

And then it hit me...

WE'RE BEST FRIENDS!

Me and Julia meshed perfectly,
and I didn't even have to do
anything to my eyebrows.

Julia and I gave each
other the freedom to be
our authentic selves.

But not everybody will do that.

Just know that they can't
see you the way *you* see you.

Because a lot of the time...
they can't even see themselves.

For example...

Me feeling my full feelings made me a great actor.

Me being really silly made me a funny comedian.

Me staying committed to my morals has made me a trusted social justice advocate.

So, anyone who doesn't want me to be my full self can

KICK

ROCKS!!

It won't always be
easy to be authentic.

Even if right now it feels really tough being you, please know it won't always be that way.

I mean it!

There are other people just
waiting to meet you and
love you for who you are.

So, the next time you feel like
everyone is heading in one direction,
but it doesn't feel right for you...

CHOOSE YOUR OWN

DIRECTION. →

The next time you feel like something doesn't feel authentic...question it.

DON'T BE AFRAID TO SPEAK UP.

When you are

YOUR AUTH

ENTIC SELF,

you give the people around you
the freedom to do the same.

Being authentic lets you decide what's cool for you.

Being authentic expands your perspective.

Being authentic **means saying no to things that aren't for you.**

Being authentic is all about being true to your emotions.

Being authentic is not about judging others.

Being authentic can be scary and full of adventure!

Every time you choose authenticity, you become more courageous.

So, **keep it real**.

BECAUSE AUTHENTICITY IS CONTAGIOUS.

And creating an authentic world...

STARTS WITH

you.

Outro
for grownups

I can't imagine being a kid in today's world. Every day, our highly impressionable young minds are being fought over by media that seeks to convince them they are not good enough.

From brands, to content, to music, trends move at the speed of light. It is our responsibility to ground our kids' blossoming identities in soil enriched with self-love and self-awareness.

I encourage us, as grownups, to encourage *them* to see not only their "best" selves, but their fullest selves. We then provide them with the lifelong gift of agency and the choice to be the change they wish to see.

About The Author

Amanda Seales is an artistic individual who creates edutainment through her independent entity, Smart Funny & Black Productions. She seamlessly weaves together the scholarship of a Master's degree in African American studies from Columbia University and an unwavering dedication to social justice, with her skill sets as a comedian, writer, visual artist, and beyond. A 30-year veteran in entertainment, she left the limelight to focus her energy on combining media, education, and artistry to shift culture, cultivate knowledge, and strengthen community. An unwavering truth translator, Ms. Seales' work walks the line of levity and gravitas, a force of nature moving steadfast toward collective liberation, by any joke necessary.

@amandaseales @amandasealesTV

Patreon.com/AmandaSeales